EARTH

All About Earthquakes, Volcanoes, Glaciers, Oceans and More

Carol Allen

Illustrated by David Pearson

Greey de Pencier Books

Published 1993 by Greey de Pencier/Books from OWL.
Books from OWL are published in Canada by Greey de Pencier Books,
56 The Esplanade, Suite 302, Toronto, Ontario M5E 1A7
All rights reserved. No part of this book may be reproduced or copied in
any form without written permission from the publisher.

Published simultaneously in the United States by Firefly Books (U.S.) Inc.
P.O. Box 1338, Ellicott Station, Buffalo, NY 14205.
Originally published in Australia by Ellsyd Press.
Copyright © 1991 text and illustrations David Ell Press Pty Ltd

*OWL and the Owl colophon are trademarks of the Young Naturalist
Foundation. Greey de Pencier Books is a licensed user of trademarks
of the Young Naturalist Foundation.

Canadian Cataloguing in Publication Data

Allen, Carol, 1947–
            Earth: all about earthquakes, volcanoes,
glaciers, oceans and more

ISBN 1-895688-06-X

1. Earth – juvenile literature. 2. Earthquakes –
Juvenile literature. 3. Volcanoes – Juvenile
literature. 4. Glaciers – Juvenile literature.
I. Pearson, David, 1947–   . II. Title.

QB631.4A55 1993   j550   C92-095064-7

Cover design: Julia Naimska
Cover photo: V. Whelan/Valan
Cover illustration: Gary Clement

Printed in Hong Kong
A   B   C   D   E   F   G

ontents

In the Beginning

Scientists believe that a huge explosion flung great clouds of hydrogen gas into the universe. Pockets of this gas began to spin around crazily, flattening into discs. Spiral arms, like bent wheel-spokes, grew until space was dotted with giant cartwheels of gas and dust whirling around. Myriads of stars began to glow and light up these **galaxies**.

Our sun and planets

About 5000 million years ago a little star began to form in the spiral arm of one galaxy. It was similar to a hundred thousand others nearby, but special to us since it was our sun.

After the sun formed, a little of the leftover gas and dust settled into a pancake-shaped cloud around it.

The dust grains jostled and stuck together, and attracted others to join them in larger lumps. These pieces of rock swept through space getting ever bigger until they grew into **planets**.

Earth is one of nine planets around the sun. **Mercury**, **Venus**, **Earth** and **Mars** are rather small rocky planets; **Pluto** probably is too. The giants of the solar system are **Jupiter**, **Saturn**, **Uranus** and **Neptune** which are really huge balls of cold, poisonous gases with just a little bit of rock in the middle.

Mercury

Venus

Earth

Mars

Jupiter

Saturn

Uranus

Neptune

Pluto

Many of them have companion moons. We have one, too, which circles us every month.

Our Earth

At first the Earth was hot and molten, but gradually the surface cooled until a thin crust formed, like skin on hot chocolate. This soon became rough and bumpy as **meteorites** — lumps of rock from space — hit it and made craters with splash marks like those you get by dropping stones into mud. Most have now worn away.

Volcanoes blew out lots of gas and water. This made a layer we call the **atmosphere**, and filled the hollows with oceans.

Our home planet is small but special: not too big or too small, not too hot or too cold, but covered in warm sea and the only planet we know of where life could begin.

Under the Skin

If you cut the Earth open what would you find?

Only one-third of Earth's surface is dry land; the rest is covered with a layer of water called the **hydrosphere**. The oceans are about 7 km (4 miles) deep on average.

Inside the Earth

The **crust** is just a thin layer of firm rock beneath our feet that stops us from sinking into the mantle. It is not one large piece but is divided into several huge blocks called **plates**. Mountains and valleys may seem very big to us, but are really only little wrinkles in the crust. The distance from the top of Mount Everest to the deepest hole in the ocean bed is less than 20 km (12 miles) — not much compared with the diameter of the whole earth which is about 12,750 km (7920 miles).

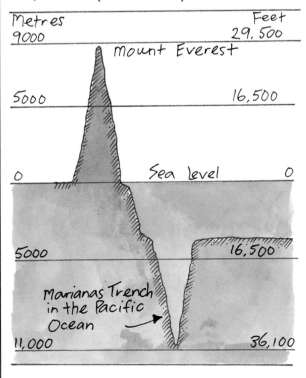

Metres		Feet
9000	Mount Everest	29,500
5000		16,500
0	Sea level	0
5000		16,500
11,000	Marianas Trench in the Pacific Ocean	36,100

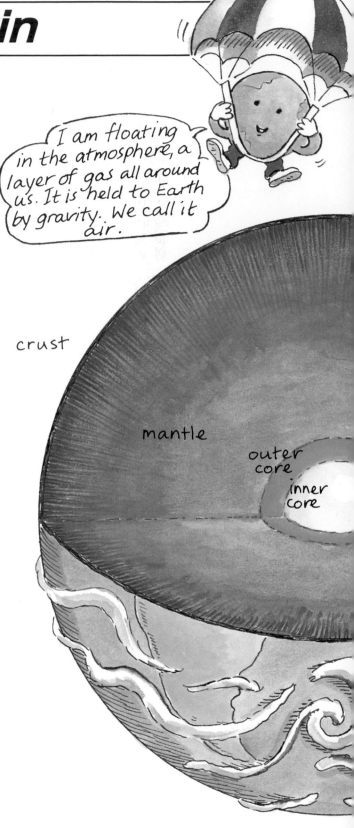

I am floating in the atmosphere, a layer of gas all around us. It is held to Earth by gravity. We call it air.

crust

mantle

outer core

inner core

Radioactive materials, like uranium, give out a lot of heat which makes the **inner core** of the Earth very hot. It is solid iron only because it is being squeezed hard by the outer layers.

The Earth turns around once each day.

The hot rock in the mantle is constantly moving in a convection cycle.

Beneath the crust is the **mantle**. This is a thick layer of hot rock which is not quite solid. It is constantly on the move as warm bits rise, cool and slowly sink at a different place. This **convection** cycle takes millions of years.

You can see the convection effect for yourself. Put some hot water in a glass jar, then gently hang a tea bag over the side until it is just covered by water (don't jiggle it!). Hold a piece of white paper behind the jar and watch the streams of tea whirl their way down and up the jar.

The convection cycle in a glass of tea

The Earth as a magnet

The **outer core** is mostly liquid iron and nickel. These hot metals swirl around as the Earth turns. Try turning a cup of water around and around and you'll make the water swirl too. When liquid iron spins it makes a magnet.

The ends of the Earth's magnet are near the North and South Poles. A compass needle points at the north end of the magnet — this is the **magnetic pole**. As the Earth's metal core slowly rotates, magnetic north moves about.

Magnetic North

True North

MAP

Only Skin Deep

The rocks of the Earth's crust are not all the same. Those under the sea floor are very heavy but only about 7 km (4 miles) thick. The continents are much deeper — between 35 to 65 km (20 to 40 miles) — but made of much lighter rock which floats on the hot mantle like crackers in thick soup.

Moving continents

Where the plates drift apart, a split opens in the crust. Hot lava wells up like blood in a cut and forms long, high, underwater mountain chains that rarely peep above the sea. The Atlantic and Pacific oceans both have them. Scientists call them **mid-ocean ridges**.

Disappearing lands

Since the Earth isn't getting bigger, when new rocks form at one edge of a plate, the opposite edge slides beneath another land block. This is called a **subduction zone** and many earthquakes occur here. When the old crust is pushed deep into the mantle, it melts and can work its way to the surface through cracks, causing volcanoes.

Japan is a chain of volcanic islands at the edge of a deep trench where the sea floor is being pushed under Asia. Some of the rock was probably scraped off the sea bottom and heaped up while volcanoes made the islands bigger.

JAPAN

Ocean Trench

moving plate

Plate starts to melt

MANTLE

SUBDUCTION ZONE

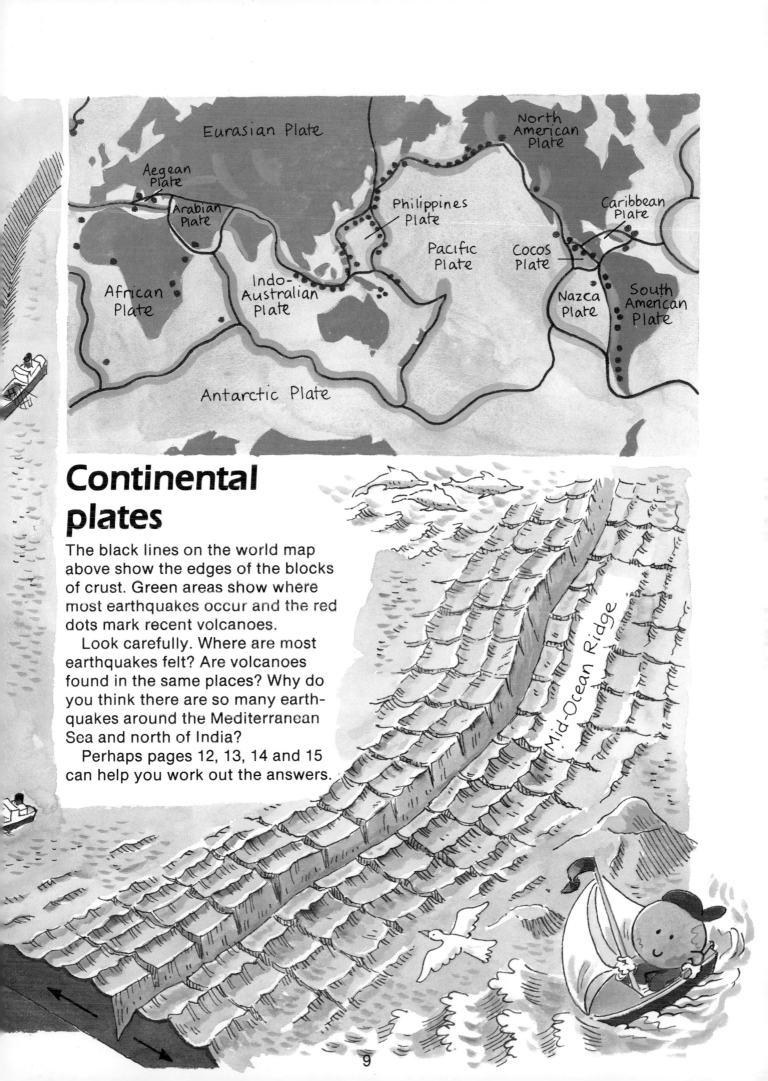

The black lines on the world map show the edges of the blocks of crust. Plate labels:

Eurasian Plate
North American Plate
Aegean Plate
Arabian Plate
Philippines Plate
Caribbean Plate
African Plate
Pacific Plate
Cocos Plate
Indo-Australian Plate
Nazca Plate
South American Plate
Antarctic Plate

Mid-Ocean Ridge

Continental plates

The black lines on the world map above show the edges of the blocks of crust. Green areas show where most earthquakes occur and the red dots mark recent volcanoes.

Look carefully. Where are most earthquakes felt? Are volcanoes found in the same places? Why do you think there are so many earthquakes around the Mediterranean Sea and north of India?

Perhaps pages 12, 13, 14 and 15 can help you work out the answers.

The Jigsaw Earth

As the hot rocks of the mantle slowly churn, the floating blocks of land are carried gradually across the Earth's surface.

Three hundred years ago Francis Bacon made a jigsaw map of the continents of North and South America and Africa, and noticed that they fitted together. Trace them from the back of the book and find out for yourself.

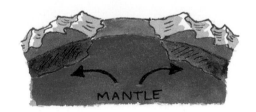

Since then, geologists have realized that some rocks and fossils on each side of the Atlantic Ocean are identical. This matching of rock layers is true in other parts of the world too, so scientists now think that all the land once formed one huge continent which they call **Pangaea**.

This split into two parts called **Laurasia** and **Gondwanaland** which began to drift apart. Laurasia went north and Gondwanaland moved south. At that time Australia was near the South Pole.

200 million years ago

135 million years ago plants began to flower for the first time

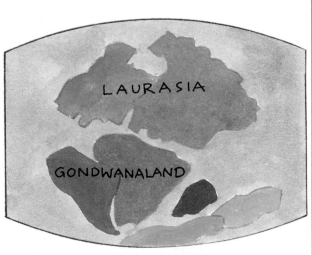

150 million years ago

10

North America broke away from Europe and Asia. Antarctica, South America, Australia, Africa and India also split apart. Antarctica remained in the cold polar regions, but the other parts of Gondwanaland headed north towards the equator.

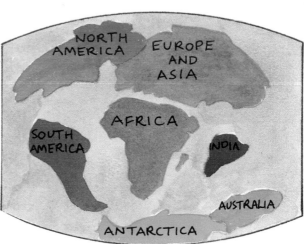

80 million years ago dinosaurs still ruled the land

India bumped into Asia, pushing up the Himalayas. Africa collided with Europe and formed the Pyrenees.

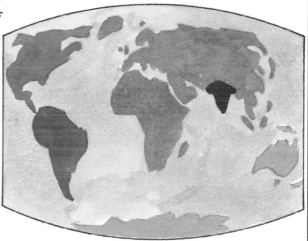

The world today

Australia is still racing north at the rate of about 7 cm (3 inches) a year. In the future Australia will lie wholly within the tropical regions.

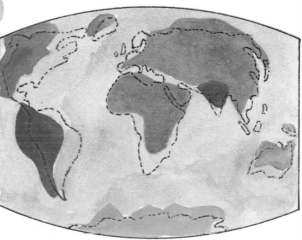

The world might look like this 50 million years in the future.

Fire Mountains

What makes a volcano?

When the hot rocks of the Earth's mantle find a crack in the crust, they spill out in fountains of fire and noisy gushes of gases and ash. In this way a **volcano** is born.

Lava is stored under a volcano in a large **magma chamber**. When it pushes hard enough, the liquid rock is forced up a crack and bursts through a **vent** to the surface in a fiery fountain of lava, ash and gas. Volcanoes on mid-ocean ridges, or the **shield volcanoes** of Hawaii, boil out great streams of thin, runny lava to build huge mountains with gently sloping sides. The rock comes from the mantle and often sets in shining waves of **pahoehoe** lava.

parasitic cone

vent

Fumaroles are holes where volcanic gases hiss out of the ground.

Diamonds may form in a pipe like this.

magma chamber

geothermal power station

geyser

hot spring

colored algae

Sometimes lava erupts from a long crack — this is a **fissure volcano**. Iceland was made in this way.

When hot rock is close to the surface, underground water is heated and bubbles up as a boiling pool. **Geysers** are like underground kettles that boil over. When there is enough steam inside one, a fountain of water is pushed up.

Iceland and New Zealand collect underground steam and use it to make electricity.

Dangerous volcanoes

Composite or **strato volcanoes** are found where crust is being pushed downwards. They have steep-sided cones made from layers of ash and lava. Their thick lava can block the vent until the force of the gas inside makes the mountain explode. A huge cloud of very hot gas and ash may rush down the slope, destroying everything in its path.

A caldera forms when the lava inside the volcano is sucked back into the Earth and the mountain top collapses, or when it is blown right off.

caldera

There are dozens of types of rock made from solidified lava. Here are two forms:

pumice   obsidian

Lava bombs are blobs of rock spat out by the volcano.

Whole forests can be blown down by a rush of hot gas.

lava tunnel

Lava streams cool on the surface first but red hot rock flows underneath. When this stops, an empty lava tunnel is left.

magma chamber

pumice raft

Volcanic rocks break down to form very fertile soil for crops to grow in. That is why people keep living close to volcanoes.

Extinct volcanoes will probably not erupt again but **dormant** ones are just resting.

Wrinkles and Cracks

Making mountains

What happens when two cars collide?

They scrunch together in wrinkles or folds, like an accordion, so they take up less space. Much the same occurs when two land blocks bump into each other. **Fold mountains**, such as the Rocky Mountains, result. You can see the effect if you shuffle your feet against the edge of a rug.

If you could cut these mountains open, you would see the layers of crumpled rock.

Sometimes rocks are squeezed so hard that they push up into the air and fold over on top of each other, forming many layers called **strata**...

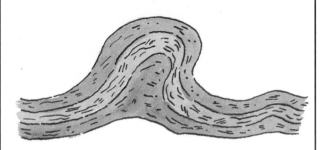

...like these.

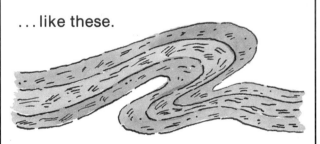

Perhaps you have seen rock layers that look like this.

This is a **fault**. If you take a wooden ruler, hold it at the ends and bend it, it will snap suddenly. Fault lines show where rocks have been pushed or pulled enough to break. Land blocks can slide up or down or beside each other, or a middle block can slip down to form a **rift valley**.

Shock waves

When the two sides of a fault suddenly slip past each other, the ground jerks. We call this an **earthquake**.

If a strong earthquake occurs near a city, thousands of people may be killed as buildings collapse and especially if fires start.

Measuring earthquakes

The strength of an earthquake is measured on the **Richter scale**. If you feel an earthquake of up to 3 or 4 on the scale, you might think it is just a big truck passing by. At 6 or 7 a lot of damage is done, and a quake of 9 would knock down almost all the buildings in a city.

Seismometers measure the strength of earthquakes. A simple type is a pen attached to a heavy weight on a wire. The weight stays still when an earthquake occurs, and as the earth wobbles under it, the pen traces a wiggly line.

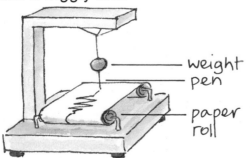

weight
pen

paper
roll

Giant waves

Tsunamis (incorrectly called tidal waves) are dangerous sea waves caused by earthquakes. On the oceans a tsunami may be only 2 m (6 feet) high, but as it runs up on land it can grow to be 40 m (130 feet) high and wash away everything in its path. Tsunamis have drowned many millions of people.

Water, Water Everywhere

The water cycle

Water in the rivers and oceans is constantly recycled. The only new water on our planet is thrown out by volcanoes which release it from the hot rocks of the mantle.

The heat of the sun turns water in the seas, lakes or soil to an invisible gas called **water vapor**. This rises high into the sky where tiny water drops form around dust grains and collect to make **clouds**.

When clouds drift over hills or mountains, they are forced upwards and get colder. Cold clouds cannot carry as much water as warm ones so the extra falls as rain or snow.

Rivers

Rainwater collects in tiny **rivulets** which run into **streams** and **rivers**. Lakes may form in hollows.

In time, as streams and rivers rush downhill, they can carve huge valleys, even through very hard rock. Heavy rains or quickly melting snow cause rivers to flood. This wears away the landscape much faster and causes damage to farmlands and cities.

Rivers carry rocks, pebbles, sand and mud from one place to another. In flat areas, rivers eat away their banks on the outside of a bend and leave sand and gravel on the inside so that the loops grow bigger. Eventually some of these **meanders** are cut off and left behind as **oxbow lakes**. At the mouth, the last of the mud and sand may make a fan-shaped **delta**.

water vapor

delta

rainfall

meander

marshy ground

oxbow lake

Underground reservoirs

Much of the rainwater soaks through the soil. If the rock below is full of tiny air spaces, it can soak up water like a sponge and hold it underground. Farmers and others can drill wells into these **aquifers** and pump the water out. In many parts of the world, such as central Australia, some wells even give hot water because of the Earth's heat.

aquifer

The Big Freeze

Ice sheets

Near the North and South Poles, the summer sun is weak and in winter it may not appear above the horizon for months at a time. Snow piles up to make great layers of ice. These **ice sheets** cover all but the highest mountains in Antarctica and float on the sea around the North Pole. Huge **icebergs** break off from these.

Near these icy regions the snow melts in summer, but except for the top 1 m (3 feet), the ground is always frozen. When the Inuit lived in igloos, they didn't need freezers; they dug a hole in the ice.

What flavor ice-block today dear, seal or whale?

Ice ages

At times in the past, the Earth was colder and ice covered much of the northern continents. These times are called **ice ages**. The last one ended about 12,000 years ago. At that time so much water turned to ice that the sea level was lower. Indonesia and the Philippines were one piece of land, and people could walk from Siberia to Alaska or from New Guinea to Australia. In fact, scientists believe that the native people of the Americas and Australia did just that.

During the ice age, glaciers cut very deep valleys. When the ice melted again the sea flooded many of them — we call them **fjords**.

icefield

lateral or side moraine

cirques are basins scooped out by ice

The polar ice sheets hold 2/3 of the world's fresh water.

when a glacier crosses a hard rock step, it breaks into jagged séracs, little pillars of ice

hanging valleys are left when glaciers cut old valleys deeper

glacier

crevasses are deep cracks in the ice

medial or middle moraine

terminal or end moraine

meltwater stream

old moraine

Glaciers

Snow falls all year round in mountain areas, even near the equator. If more falls than melts, **icefields** grow and hollows fill with snow. Eventually a river of ice begins to slide down to the valleys below. These **glaciers** slowly grind their way through the toughest rock to carve out huge valleys that have steep sides and a flat floor.

Glaciers gouge out enormous amounts of rock, and more falls on them from cliffs broken by frost. As the glacier melts, this rock rubbish is left at the sides and snout as heaps called **moraines**. A river usually takes the **meltwater** away. It often looks milky since the ice can grind rock to a fine powder like flour.

Filling in the Hollows

Erosion

Plate collisions and volcanoes create new mountains which at once start to wear away. Hot sun, water, ice, wind and plants all help to break rocks apart. These start the process of **erosion**.

In deserts, hot days and cold nights weaken rock faces. Flash floods and high winds move rocks, soil and sand, depositing them in another place. Windblown sand can carve arches in rock slabs and wear away boulders to a mushroom shape.

Sand is often blown into piles called **dunes**. Some are crescent- or star-shaped, others form in long waves.

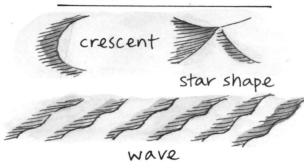

Sand Dune Patterns

crescent

star shape

wave

In colder areas, water seeps into tiny cracks in the rocks. When it freezes it takes up more space and pushes the little crack wider until, in time, a piece of rock falls off. A glacier or stream may carry it down towards the sea, constantly rubbing it smaller. Rivers can round jagged boulders to little pebbles as they roll along the bottom.

The Life Story of Bertie Boulder

In flat areas, rivers drop their rock load to form flat **flood plains**. At the mouth, sea currents may carry sand away to build **beaches**.

Water also dissolves some types of rock such as chalk or limestone. The chemicals are carried into the sea where tiny animals use them to make hard shells. When the animals die, the shells drift to the bottom to make more limestone. After millions of years the layers of the sea bed may be pushed up as new land.

Over many millions of years the great mountain ranges of the world erode to become someone else's sand dunes. The land becomes flatter until the Earth moves again to push up new mountains which again begin to wear down.

Try using a hose to make erosion patterns in piles of sand and gravel. Does a water jet give the same kind of pattern as a sprinkler?

tube coral
brain coral
hard coral
gorgonian sea fan

Coral reefs are huge cities of limestone built by tiny animals. They construct their homes on underwater mountains to be close to the sunlight. It has taken about a million years to form the Great Barrier Reef this way.

Fossils: Casts from the Past

Fossils are the remains of animals and plants preserved in rock.

Once, long ago, a mother trachodon, guarding her eggs and babies, was attacked and killed by a fearsome tyrannosaurus rex. He gobbled his lunch and left the half-eaten carcass.

Over many years, minerals carried in by water turned the bones to stone.

Sand blew over the nest and bones and hid them from the sun, rain and other animals.

For millions of years, the bones stayed hidden underground. Then the landscape changed and a river began to eat into the rock above them until they peeped out of the bank.

Sometimes the animal or plant rotted away but left a **cast** of its shape behind. You can make a cast of a shell by pressing it into modelling clay. If you fill the hole with wet plaster, you can peel the clay off your plaster "fossil" when it is dry.

Very rarely, animals are buried alive and their smallest details preserved. Fossils of these creatures show skin, eyes, insect feelers and even the color scales of a butterfly's wings.

5 A paleontologist, a scientist who studies fossils, saw the bones and dug them out using heavy hammers and chisels.

6 The bones were carefully numbered and wrapped in wet plaster bandages which hardened to protect them. They were then taken to a museum.

7 Here the bones were cleaned, sorted and put together in the right order to make a skeleton of the trachodon which was mounted on a steel stand.

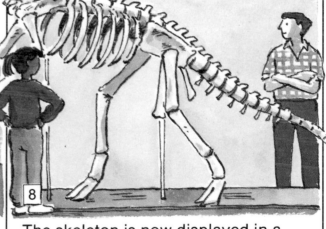

8 The skeleton is now displayed in a museum gallery where people can study it and understand what the animal looked like 70 million years before they were born.

The fossilized feather of ARCHAEOPTERYX, the first bird.

By looking at the fossils found in rocks, scientists have worked out how life forms changed from the first tiny cells to the human body — one of nature's newest inventions.

Clocks in the Rocks

We can picture the whole history of the Earth as a twelve-hour clock face. About 4600 million years ago the Earth was formed. Over the next 1000 million years volcanoes, sunlight and lightning changed some of the atmosphere to new kinds of chemicals that clung together. Life probably began from these chemicals as tiny blobs of jelly lurking in the dark mud at the bottom of the sea 3500 million years ago.

These simple **bacteria** bred so well that they ran out of room and had to start moving up into the light where some of them made a green-colored chemical called **chlorophyll**. Using sunshine and water, the green blobs made their own food. These **algae** were the first plants. The green slimes you see in streams or dirty swimming pools are types of algae.

Other life forms found it easier to eat their neighbors. All animals, including us, are descended from them.

At first each living thing was just one tiny cell, but between 10 and 11 on our clock face these strung together to make the first seaweeds and sponges. Many of the shells, corals, anemones and jellyfish that you can find along the beaches today have changed very little since their ancestors first appeared.

Many different types of bacteria live happily inside your body. "Good" ones help you digest your food but "bad" ones make you sick.

THIS IS OUR GEOLOGICAL CLOCK

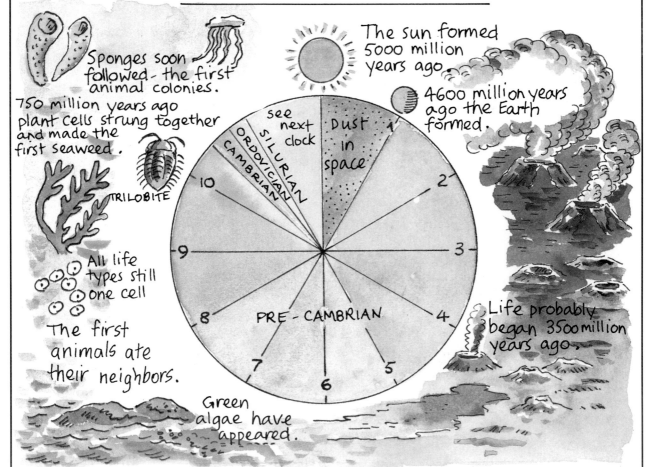

Sponges soon followed - the first animal colonies.

750 million years ago plant cells strung together and made the first seaweed.

TRILOBITE

All life types still one cell

The first animals ate their neighbors.

Green algae have appeared.

The sun formed 5000 million years ago.

4600 million years ago the Earth formed.

Life probably began 3500 million years ago.

Dust in space

PRE - CAMBRIAN

CAMBRIAN
ORDOVICIAN
SILURIAN

see next clock

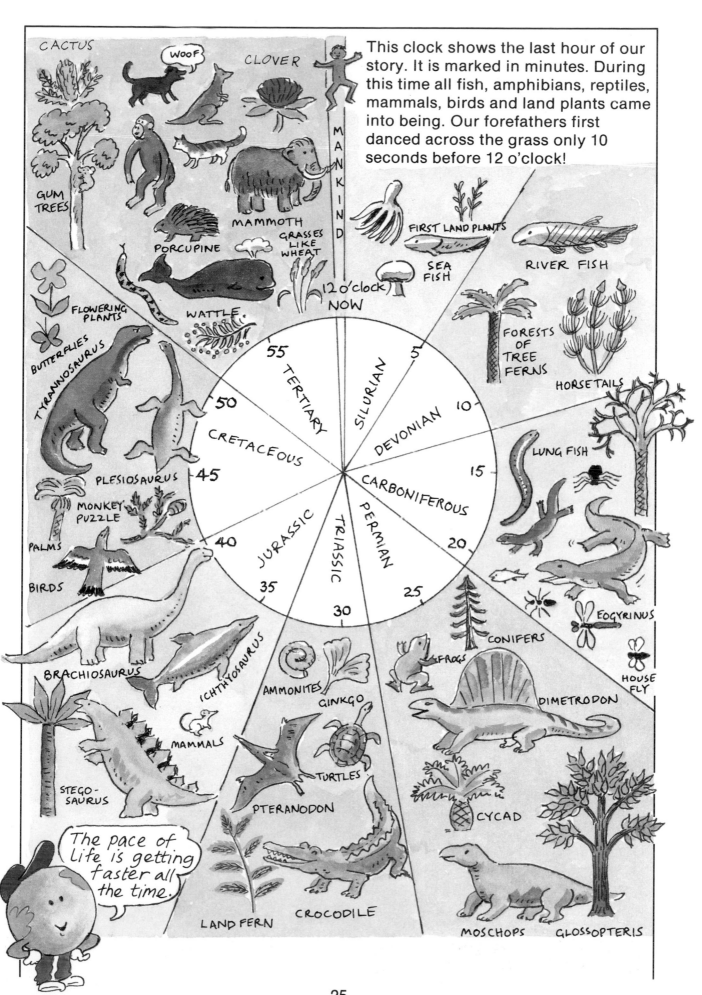

This clock shows the last hour of our story. It is marked in minutes. During this time all fish, amphibians, reptiles, mammals, birds and land plants came into being. Our forefathers first danced across the grass only 10 seconds before 12 o'clock!

_T_he Breath of Life

How the air changed

When the Earth was young the air was poisonous. Green-colored cells used carbon dioxide, sunshine and water to make food, and gave off oxygen. Over many millions of years the atmosphere changed into what we enjoy today. Most of the air is nitrogen but one-fifth is oxygen which animals need for breathing. There is also a small amount of carbon dioxide which plants use to make food. If there had never been plants, we could not live on Earth.

The greenhouse effect

Every time we light the barbecue, use a car or burn coal to make electricity, a bit more carbon dioxide floats into the sky. Many scientists think that too much of this gas will act like a blanket around the Earth and make it hotter. This is known as the **greenhouse effect**. The polar ice could melt and cause the sea level to rise and flood many cities. If the weather became too hot, deserts would spread and we would be unable to grow enough food to eat.

To avoid this, people must use less fuel. We can all help by walking and using buses, trains or bicycles instead of cars. Are you helping our world by walking or riding your bicycle to school?

Pardon me! Burp

Layers in the air

The air near the Earth's surface is wet and fairly warm. If you went up in a balloon, you would find that it gets colder the further you rise.

The air above us is in several layers. One acts like a mirror for radio waves so that we can bounce radio signals off it to distant places on Earth.

Radio waves bounced from the Ionosphere

Ozone and us

Far above us is a layer of **ozone** gas. This is oxygen that has been changed by the fierce rays of the sun. Ozone traps many of the sun's harmful rays. Without it, both plants and animals would die. There is now at least one hole in the ozone layer which may have been caused by chemicals. It is located over Antarctica, but sometimes moves over Australia, where people may get skin cancer from being out in the sun too much. There may also be a hole growing over the Arctic and North America.

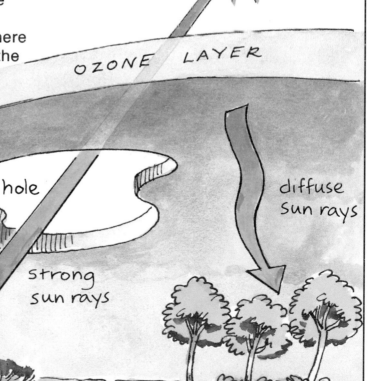

Our World

Caring for our world

Every day our world is changed a little more, sometimes on purpose and sometimes by accident. Unfortunately it often changes in a bad way: the world you will grow up in will not be as beautiful a place unless we all learn to be more careful.

Think about the following questions. Find out more. Write letters to politicians to tell them what you think. It's *your* world too.

Mining and quarrying scar the land and produce ugly piles of waste. The underground tunnels can cave in and undermine homes or factories. Should mining companies be asked to fill in old tunnels with waste rock?

Clearcutting of forests destroys their natural beauty, drives animals from their homes, and lets the soil wash away so it is hard for new trees to grow. Should we let this go on, or should we use less paper and recycle it, while finding better ways to harvest the trees that we need from our forests?

Forests attract rain. Felling them spreads deserts. Trees are now being chopped down faster than they can grow again. Every person needs about 25 trees to make the oxygen they breathe each year. When did you last plant a tree?

Fires destroy many trees, plants, crops and animals. Are you careful not to drop matches or bottles that might start a fire?

Clearing land and hunting for food or sport have made many animals extinct. One more type disappeared forever while you were reading this sentence. Should these activities be better controlled?

Farming is very hard work? To earn enough money it's tempting to put more animals on a farm than is good for the ground. If the animals eat grass faster than it grows, the land becomes bare and soil blows away. Should city people pay more for farm products so that farmers don't have to overstock their land?

River life is killed if too much mud washes into the water or if farmers use too many chemicals to kill off weeds or insects. Should we fine polluters more, and make better laws to protect the rivers?

Dirt roads are cheaper to build than paved ones, but they increase erosion. Should motorists pay more to build better roads?

People who live in dry places have to pump water out of the ground. They are using water faster than the aquifers refill. In 20 years most of the wells will be dry. What will thirsty humans and animals drink then?

Did you know that loss of top soil is the worst environmental problem in the world? Without good soil, crops will fail.

Problems of Pollution

This is the only world we have, but what are we doing to it?

Pollutants are things which spoil the world for others. How many can you see in this picture?

Can you find things which are good for our environment?

Remember: if you don't NEED it, don't buy it. If you must buy it, try to recycle it.

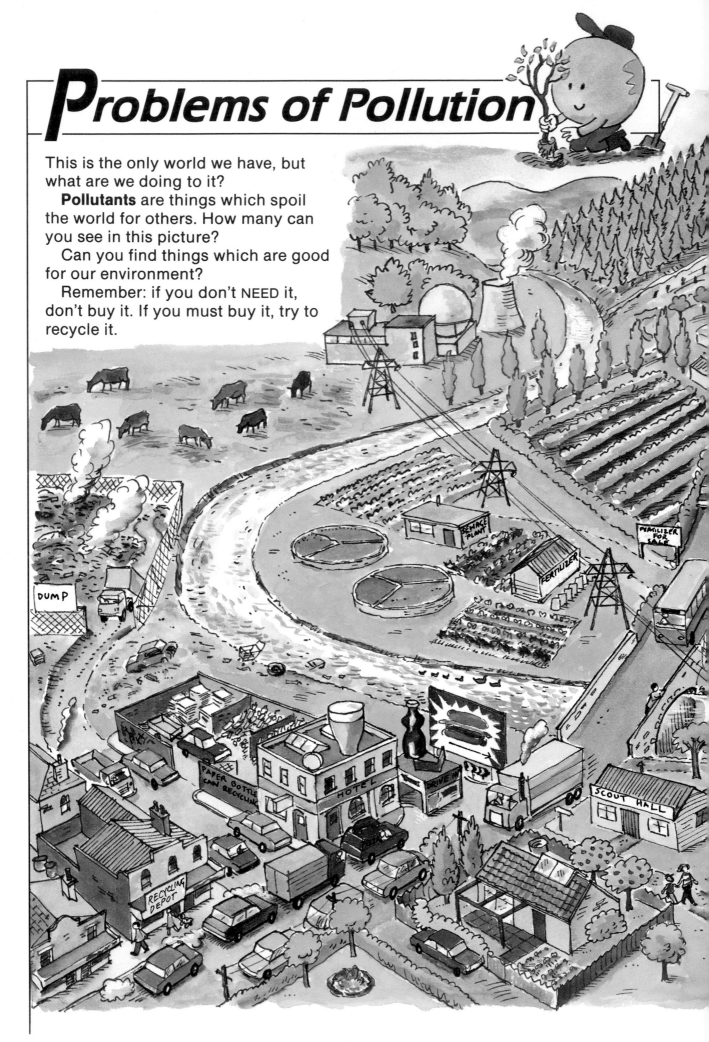

Puzzling

Here are some jigsaw pieces. If you trace them on paper you can cut them out and fit them together to look like the maps of the ancient Earth on pages 8 and 9.

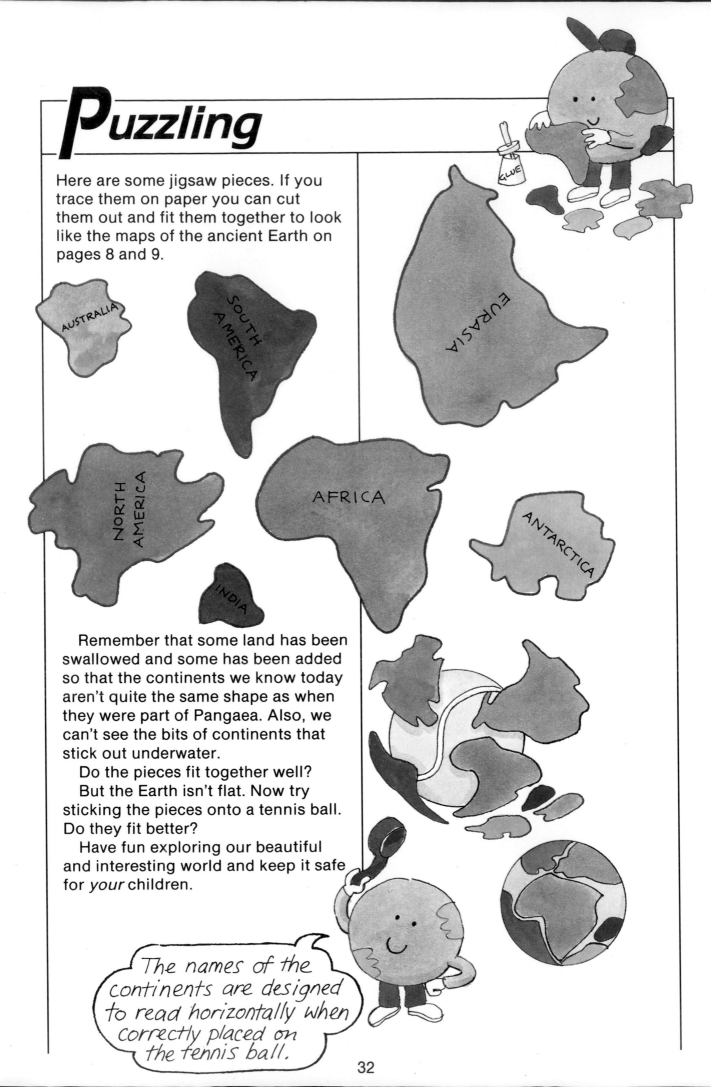

AUSTRALIA

SOUTH AMERICA

EURASIA

NORTH AMERICA

AFRICA

ANTARCTICA

INDIA

Remember that some land has been swallowed and some has been added so that the continents we know today aren't quite the same shape as when they were part of Pangaea. Also, we can't see the bits of continents that stick out underwater.

Do the pieces fit together well?

But the Earth isn't flat. Now try sticking the pieces onto a tennis ball. Do they fit better?

Have fun exploring our beautiful and interesting world and keep it safe for *your* children.

The names of the continents are designed to read horizontally when correctly placed on the tennis ball.